GHOST TOWN ALMANAC

By

Thomas D. Reynolds

ACKNOWEDGEMENTS

Alabama Literary Review (No. 12, 1996-1997)
"Everything is a Fossil"
New Delta Review (Vol. 14, Number 1, Fall/Winter 1996)
"Happy Hour at Vera's"
Aethlon: The Journal of Sport Literature (XIII: Spring 1996)
"Report From the Battle"
Aethlon: The Journal of Sport Literature (XVIII: 1, Fall 1999)
"Three Versions of Cap Evans' Pool Hall"
Aethlon: The Journal of Sport Literature (XXI: 2, Spring 2004)
"Rodeo"
Aethlon: The Journal of Sport Literature (XXII: 2, Spring 2005)
"The Bottom" (the first three stanzas published as "Strip Pit Fishing")
Aethlon: The Journal of Sport Literature (XXIII:2, Spring 2006)
"The Bottom" (the last three stanzas published as "Rock Climbing in Horse Thief Canyon")
American Western Magazine (October 2003 issue)
"Chadwell, Miller, and Pitts"
Midwest Poetry Review (July, 1997)
"Land of the Post Rock"
The MacGuffin (Vol. XVIII, No. 1, Spring 2001)
"Quarry Murder Mystery"
Potpourri (Vol. 15, No. 3, Fall 2003)
"Love Poem"
Wings Online (January 9, 2005)
"The Lost World"
*Ken*again* (Vol. 5, No. 2, Summer 2004)
"Barker"
"Skippy the Wonder Rock"
Sidereality (Vol. 3, Issue 2, June 2004)
"Doomsday"
Farsight Magazine (May Edition, 2005)
"The Past"
The Pedestal Magazine (Twenty-Eighth Issue—June 21-August 21, 2005)
"The Hard-Boiled Paleontologist"
Flint Hills Review (Issue Nine, 2004)
"How to Hunt Fossils"

Persistent Mirage (Issue No. 5, June 2005)
"Wizard of Wheels"
"Raisins"
Muscadine Lines: A Southern Journal (Volume #4, July/August 2005)
"Delmer"
Poetry Midwest (Spring/Summer 2004)
"Find Me a Stone" (published under the title "Stone")
Thieves Jargon (March 17, 2006)
"Jackrabbit Drive"
American Western Magazine (February 2004)
"Sunday Morning on Main Street"
A Man Overboard (October 2004)
"Long Live Rock!"
2River View (9.4, Summer 2005)
"Bluegrass"
"Trap"
American Western Magazine (July 23, 2004)
"Black Sheep"
Voltaire's Inkwell (Volume 1, Issue 1, April 2006)
"Birth of a Temporary Town"
Prairie Poetry (Summer 2005)
"An Expatriate Kansan Rides the Train of Remembering"
Prairie Poetry (October 2004)
"A Tour of Bloom"
Prairie Poetry (May 2004)
"Corps of Discovery"
Prairie Poetry (December 2005)
"Burning the Fields"
Prairie Poetry (March 2004)
"Mental Notes of a Kansas Hermit"
The Pedestal Magazine (Issue 24, 2004)
"The Day I Became an Exile"
3rd Muse Poetry Journal (Issue 28, March-April 2004)
"Hopi Maiden with Squash-Blossom Hairdress"
Ariga (January-February, 2004)
"Journey"
New Verse News (December 21, 2005)
"No. 102"
Megaera (Vol. 8, Issue 3, No. 26, Summer 2006)
"The Geographic Center"

Ash Canyon Review (2004)
"The Blizzard of 1888"
Arsenic Lobster Poetry Journal (Issues 8, 9, and 10, Summer 2006)
"Hog Heaven"
Muscadine Lines: A Southern Journal (Vol. #6, November/December 2005)
"Wanda's Fried Chicken"
Thick with Conviction (October 2005, Issue 1)
"Tiptoe Through the Tombstones"
Noo Journal (Autumn 2005)
"January Train"
Kansas Voices: Winning Entries from the Second Five Years, 1995-1999
"Fossil Hunters"

Poems Reprinted from the chapbook *Electricity*. Ed. Cynthia Pederson and Celia Daniels. Topeka, Kansas: Ligature Press, 1987.
"Intro"
"Wizard of Wheels"
"Electricity"
"Raisins"
"Fishing on the Kaw River Rule"

The poems "Happy Hour at Vera's" and "Doomsday" are based on photographs and journal entries in the book *The Pioneer Spirit* by Lyle Alan White.

TABLE OF CONTENTS

I. THE BOOK OF STONES

The Past 3
How to Hunt Fossils 5
Fossil Hunters 9
Journey 13
Love Poem 14
Quarry Murder Mystery 15
The Lost World 18
The Bottom 20
Skippy the Wonder Rock 22
Find Me a Stone 24
Long Live Rock! 26
The Hard-Boiled Paleontologist 28
Everything is a Fossil 31

II. GHOST TOWN ALMANAC

Corps of Discovery 35
The Founder of Our Town 36
Report from the Battle 38
Birth of a Temporary Town 39
Sunday Morning on Main Street 41
Black Sheep 43
Chadwell, Miller, and Pitts 45
Jackrabbit Drive 46
Land of the Post Rock 48
Bluegrass Till Dawn 49
The Blizzard of 1888 50
Three Versions of Cap Evans' Pool Hall 52
Hope Maiden with Squash Blossom Hairdress 54
Prairie Phantom 55
Mental Notes of a Kansas Hermit 56
The Day I Became an Exile 57
Barker 59
Ghost Town Almanac 60

III. HAPPY HOUR AT VERA'S

Intro 69
Raisins 70
Happy Hour at Vera's 72
Fishing on the Kaw River Rule 74
Tiptoe Through the Tombstones 75
January Train 76
Doomsday 78
Delmer 79
Wanda's Fried Chicken 81
Wizard of Wheels 83
Long Day at Muddy Creek 84
Trap 86
A Tour of Bloom 87
Rodeo 89
Burning the Fields 90
Electricity 91
Hog Heaven 93
No. 102 95
The Geographic Center 97
An Expatriate Kansan Rides the Train of Remembering 99

I. THE BOOK OF STONES

THE PAST

The range of hills at the edge of our home
Was once the home to Indians,
Living along rock bluffs
Of Ottawa Creek.
Names of the past,
Distanced by worlds of change,
Survive,
And our lives rest in shadows
And language of those wanderers.

We glance down at our feet,
Whether in plowed fields,
Or walking among hedge trees
Along the creek bank,
And pieces of rock,
Slivers of flint,
Glow in dust,
And we take them in shaking hands,
Rubbing dirt away,
Shining them with spit,
And whisper softly,
As if in prayer,
The name of our town,

Oswego.

We cannot claim a heritage not ours.
We slowly gather in our rooms
small collections of fragments,
The piece of what appears to be human bone,
Broken particles of clay,
The tip of a flawed arrowhead.
But we do not fool ourselves.

Fragments left from their earthly time,
Left from their earthly time,
Names we use,

Are only the most tentative of connections,
As when the plane circling low above us,
Gliding in a distant universe of light and air,
Waves its wings at us below in the fields,
Descends over smoky hills,
And lands
Out of sight.

HOW TO HUNT FOSSILS

"It is up to every fossil collector to behave in such a way that we will always be welcome."

June Culp Zeitner

1. Seek areas
Where few people
Are found, solitary
Deserted places,
Anywhere there is under-
Brush. Try the Flint Hills,
If possible. And dry creek
Beds, ravines, dumps, ghost
Towns, stone piles. Always stop
At roadcuts. These ugly
Barren places, cut off from
The world, know what it feels
Like to be underappreciated.
They will surround you. There
You will be yourself.

2. Always take a
Friend, if you can,
Someone to share the long
Jeep ride into the hills.
Never stray far from those
Footsteps in the rocks. Even
If you can't see your friend,
Those sounds will comfort you.
And if you are ever hurt, or
You find some gorgeous strain
In the shale, maybe sea lilies,
With their delicate petals,
Shout, and your friend will
Come running. Shouting is good
For you.

3. Vehicles are
Important, the means
By which you arrive at
Your destination. The roads
You travel may be rough.
Those back country trails can
Do a number on your shocks.
Older models with sturdy frames
Are best, not too flashy
But dependable. Jeeps are
Great. Choose the vehicle that
Best suits your needs, and then
Drive all you want, observing
All rules of the road. Don't forget
To check your tire pressure.

4. Be careful.
Move at once if
Rocks begin falling
Overhead. Wear gloves,
And a brimmed hat
To protect your eyes.
If your jeep is disabled far
From towns or farms or
Main roads, stay with
The vehicle, especially
In rugged weather. If a twister
Seems imminent, head
For the nearest ditch.
They come on quickly some-
Times, cruel and unforgiving.

5. Work slowly,
Methodically. This
Is not an Olympic event.
If digging in a shale
Pit, peel away the layers
One by one. Never be
Discouraged by lack
Of results. Searching is
The important thing,
Regardless of finds.

When they come, terrific.
If not, keep on. Don't
Be fooled by the glittery
And bright. The rough dry
And brittle hold the greatest
Rewards. Onward.

6. Respect fences.
They were put there
For a reason. So were
The no trespassing signs.
If you are still determined
To hunt in such an area, be
Careful. If possible, talk
With the owners. They may know
Where the best finds are located,
But have no interest in them.
This doesn't mean they couldn't
See the value in them, but only
That they've never been shown. How
Beautiful is the overlooked!

7. Take plenty of
Notes. When out on
The hunt, keep a record
Of findings you make,
Small things,
Seemingly insignificant,
Surrounding materials, other
Fossils discovered nearby,
Colors or discolorations,
Strange markings in the rocks.
Interesting connections can
Be made later, when the heat
Of discovery passes, when
Passion of the collector gives
Way to the reasoning insight
Of the artist.

8. Handle them
Carefully, as if they
Were your own imprints,

The only traces of your
Existence left on earth.
If the fossils are broken,
Wrap the pieces in aluminum
Foil, and place them in a
Small box or bag. At the end
Of the day, set them with
The others on the car seat,
And drive home. Finally,
Everything is alive—you, your friend,
The past, the future,
In the rocks, in the air, and in the earth.

FOSSIL HUNTERS

We walked the dry creek bed's course,
Looking over stones for fossils,
Which we chiseled out of rock
And wrapped in aluminum foil.
We walked in silence, for that
Was our agreement that year,
Unspoken and yet never broken,
If possible. The hours passed
With only our footsteps conversing
Among timber. Carp that once prowled that
Space were ghosts, if anything,
Gasping in dead air.
While I worked over a strain
Of coral engraved in a flat rock,
Father walked ahead, shoulders
Hunched to the cold,
Until he disappeared.
The creek's body was gone,
Only a dark imprint left,
A jagged scar in the earth
We endlessly trekked, searching.

We sometimes walked near
The dam of Hillsdale Lake,
Climbing over boulders on the shore.
The water's weight pressed
Against the sand, waves
Covering fossils of snail shells
With fine spray. In that lake,
In a far cove, two brothers
Drowned, dying in each other's arms,
One paralyzed, the other
Unwilling to let his brother go,
And save himself, condemned
By the bond of brotherhood.
The fields and towns were buried
By waves, the whole valley alive

Only in photographs of the past.
When we dug out fossils from rock,
We tossed stone chippings
Into the dark lake, silently,
One by one, until they were gone.

The stench of garbage,
Diapers and food scraps,
Blew from the dark pit,
Stinging our nostrils.
We backed the truck to the edge,
And began unloading,
Barrels of bottles and cans,
Decrepit chairs, broken lamps,
Bits of our existence.
Father hesitated before tossing
Away his old coat,
Which flapped in the wind, arms
Flailing, until it struck bottom,
Spread out like the corpse
Of a broken man. We kicked
Stray items along the edge,
Hoping for a bit of gold,
Before it would all be gathered up,
Bulldozed under, covered by layers
Of earth, made sacred by ritual.

While gathering walnuts in the hills,
We dug through piles of stones
Uncovered by plows seining
Through dark sod.
Meteorites, or pieces of them,
Were known to turn up in fields,
Marked by their final impact.
Ice once tore across this landscape,
Dragging its length over frozen earth,
A slow, tired journey of thousands
Of years, that leveled mountains,
Transforming rugged features
Into a mask of faceless depression.
With heavier stones, we lifted

Them together, examining undersides,
As if our lives counted
On such discoveries. We may have
Even believed that, as we grieved over
Stones arranged in piles like graves.

The truck stalled just as
The rain picked up,
Rolling in dark ribbons
Across the windshield.
We coasted next to a roadcut,
Ripped by dynamite
Through massive hills.
Cars swam in air that was
But shadow of rock.
Father worked over the engine,
Rain coursing over his face,
Down his back, baptizing him
While he bent to check the plugs.
I poured over rocks,
Letting rain wash away
The sweat of the day,
Examining the ledge for finds
I might have missed altogether
If we hadn't been driving this road,
And the truck hadn't stalled,
Near this spot, and rain
Hadn't felt so good.

The rock quarry was abandoned,
Guarded by cranes
Frozen into gaunt positions.
The crude pit was where
The best finds were located,
Arisen by dynamite from stone graves,
Dolomite crystals, scouring rushes,
Coral pieces agatized into gems.
We peered over remains,
Animals and plants that once thrived
Under dark oceans. Our picks and shovels
Rang out with renewed vigor,
My father on a high ledge

Surrounded by boulders,
While I dug in a shale pit.
We labored as if we thought
We were really going to find something,
The past, some answers, any truth,
The origin of our sadness.
We would keep on working until
One of us discovered the stone,
Laying down his pick,
Shouting, "Found it!

JOURNEY

With a pick,
You loosen it
From stone.

In your hand,
The fossil is gray, pitted,
Whorled like a spring,
A cocoon ready
To open.

Protected inside
The rock shelf for
Five million years,
It is now at your mercy,
Suddenly vulnerable,
Fragile boat
In the sea of your hand.

Lest you feel strong,
It is older than you,
And wiser. It has passed
Through death, a gradual
Flow like sand or water,
Into a dark endless ocean.

For days,
You've stood on this ledge,
Pacing the rim, like the bride
Of an explorer searching
For sails on the horizon.

Brave sailor
Clinging to its raft of rock,
Washed ashore after
A violent storm. Now you
Enfold it like a lonely spouse
Who never gave up hope,
A tender but selfish caress.

LOVE POEM

You can't swim in a river
Weighted by stones,
A slab of granite
Around each ankle,
Thrown from a bridge
In the dark of night.

You can't pull a trailer
Up a canyon road
If it's filled with rocks,
Large oblong fragments
Speckled with quartzite
Crashing from side to side.

But weighted by stones,
Gulping river water,
I'd still be glad I refused
To finger you to the mob,
The blond blue-eyed dame
Who iced Big Boy Dupree.

On the lip of Bryce Canyon,
Radiator billowing steam
And transmission shot,
I'd still be glad I married you,
The quaint house in the hills
And your rock garden dreams.

QUARRY MURDER MYSTERY

The body was discovered
On a slab of sandstone
Of the Dakota formation,
At the quarry's north end.
The stone is brownish,
Cemented by iron oxide
With a range of colors:
Yellow, purple, brown,
And now (the detective
Swabs at a wide stain)
A darkening blood red.

The body of a young girl
Inanimate as stone,
White as pure limestone,
Bruised about the neck,
Tangled like a weed
Sprouting from a crack,
Blood spreading out
Like growing branches.
In the tangle of hair,
A human expression
The detective can't bear.

He stares at a boulder
Newly blasted from rock,
Trying to fit its shape
Back onto the rock face
Like an oblong puzzle piece,
Eyes shifting from boulder
Back to the rock face,
Becoming as frustrated
As he had as a child
Laboring over pieces
Of the Grand Canyon.

He thinks of dynamite
Tearing rocks from walls.

Hundreds of tons of stone
Forced from the earth
In a few huge pieces.
He imagines a blast now,
Possibly at his feet,
Sparing him from glancing
Back at the small body
Positioned on the rock
Like a disheveled fossil.

Staring into rock,
Wishing he were a geologist
Instead of a detective,
He imagines the force
That tore her loose
And sent her crashing
Onto this pile of stone.
A force less explosive
But equally relentless,
That dissolves rock
Or separates continents.

A paleontologist would study
The fragmented fossil,
Extracting it from rock
With a scientist's love,
Bestowing on the remains
A thousand small attentions,
Bonding as if she were
A million years extinct,
A perfect leaf imprint
Or fly trapped in amber.

A geologist would examine
The stratas of stone,
The possible interbedding
Of shale with sandstone,
Puzzling over this fact
As if it were a clue,
The indispensable clue
Linking suspect to crime.
Samples will be gathered

To confirm the time,
Cretaceous or Triassic.

Then a link will be found.
"The killer or killers
of this little girl,"
the paleontologist says,
"has taken other victims."
And he'll scan the rocks
With pick and chisel,
Uncovering evidence
Of a possible serial killer.
"I'll need my microscope,"
he'll say, "and my slides."

The geologist, meanwhile,
Will narrow the timeline,
A span of ten million years
In which the victims died.
A large chunk of sandstone
Will sit on his lab table
For weeks, then months.
"The identity of the culprit
resides in this stone,"
the geologist will insist,
conducting test after test.

But the investigation stalls,
Tapers off, and disappears,
Becomes a trivial footnote
In *Paleontology Today*.
Haunted by the little girl,
The geologist takes the case
Of a woman who vanished
On a gravel road in Tulsa.
"I need a large search party,"
he tells the local detective,
"and every stone examined."

THE LOST WORLD

Walking along the creek,
We collected shells
Of snails and mussels,
And prodded fading carcasses
Of dead carp, nearly translucent,
Washed up along the bank.
With pistols carefully poised,
We fired at sticks
Swirling downstream
And rusty cans and dark splashes
Of unknown life.
With stilled hearts
We hesitated above the ripple
Of a snake's trail
As it stalked prey among
Crags and overhanging limbs.
Beavers stripped bark from
The tallest trees, and giant turtles
Gripped tenaciously onto lines
We set over the deepest spots.
We caught sight of the great blue heron,
Beating primeval wings,
Reconnoitering over hedge trees,
A lonely figure of terror
And watchfulness and wonder.
We slowly gathered in our rooms
Small collections of fossils,
Frightening images of lost worlds,
Bizarre arrays of arms
and legs that once crawled
Along the bottom of the great prairie ocean.
After a long swim in the creek,
Our arms and legs sometimes still
Felt like they were underwater,
Even on the long walk home,
As if the ocean still covered the ravines,
And the rock bluffs and ponds,
Though we could still breathe, and we crept

Over those hills like primeval beings
Transformed, as if we had been
Living this way all our lives,
And might one day be fossils,
If we were lucky.

THE BOTTOM

Near Pleasanton,
Strip pits of a defunct coal-mining operation,
Hidden from the road by thick woods
And tall rock fences,
Grow darker with every rain,
Every avalanche of dirt and rock
From towering walls.
Dynamite blasts,
Nearly fifty years old,
Still echo from rock bluffs,
And small reverberations
Still send fragments
Scurrying into deep pits.

We drive these roads,
Scarred by wheels of coal trucks,
Through stinkweed,
Down the only level approach to the water.
Lowering the boat,
We coast onto the choppy surface,
Marred by wind,
And maneuver around the crooked fingers
Of the pit's edge.
The steady rumble of the motor
Crawls along the cliffs,
As if another boat follows our movements
From the opposite shore.

We don't catch anything.
The bass hide among drowned rocks,
Prowling secret hollows.
When they surface,
Finally arisen in death,
It won't be our hooks
Their scaly jaws grasp.
When we lower the anchor,
The endless expanse of rope,

It goes down, down,
And dangles above the bottom.

We pull the boat ashore
Along a rock bank
Made up of fallen boulders
Scattered with frail beginnings of cottonwoods.
Our boots clatter along stones,
Our hands caress brittle layers
Of shale deposits,
Engraved with fossils,
Which crumble at the softest touch,
Turn to dust.

The steep cliff,
Layers of millions of years,
Carefully preserved,
Slowly flakes away
Or falls in great blocks,
Shattering below.
Each stratum leads to another,
All the way to the tall weeds,
The overhanging elm,
At the bluff's summit.

We can't climb it,
Even with the proper gear,
We tell ourselves,
Stuck here at the bottom,
The lowest rung,
Primitive men,
Backs to water,
Eyeing those precarious crags.

SKIPPY THE WONDER ROCK

So what if you're a mutt,
Mostly a coarse gray breed
Mixed with white flint,
Dotted with clear quartzite
(one of your grandparents?),
mud clinging to your belly.
You've been a faithful rock,
Patient beyond understanding.

My daughter saw you at the park,
Subject to a subliminal charm
That escaped me, I'll admit.
Wait for this to grow on me?
Hell, I won't live that long.
But you exist on a higher plain,
Your hum fills a dark room,
One continuous sublime bark.

Definitely low maintenance,
I'll say that on your behalf.
Though you fell from the chair
Once, carelessly brushing my hand.
I glued the two pieces together,
Patted your reptilian back,
Muttered, "good boy, good boy,"
And set you on your perch.

Your unwillingness to please
Is rivaled only by a cat's,
Diffidence and cool unconcern.
Your best trick is playing dead,
Which you've got down cold.
With a little assistance,
You can sit up or roll over,
But you could never beg. No.

We don't have the good times
Other pets and owners have,

The playful give and take.
Sometimes I feel I should
Hug you in the crook of my arm
And lay a noogie on you.
Now get yourself over here,
My petrified chicken liver.

If a cat has nine lives,
How many do you possess?
And exactly what is the ratio
Of human vs. rock years?
For every year of human life,
Times it by twelve million?
In which case I'm real old,
You arrogant pup.

Soon you'll have to face
The inevitable deterioration,
The slow stumbling walk,
A mind racing ever faster
Over hills it once roamed.
My passing could be eased
By a succession of owners.
Just wait a century or two,

That's all I ask.
Oh, the times we've had,
You asleep on the table,
Me spilling crumbs on you,
But you never complained,
Never offered to desert.
Forget Frisbees or ball.
Let's just sit here awhile.

FIND ME A STONE

Bending down to pick up a flint
Just as my daughter calls out,
A swirling red and white marvel
With several frail black threads
And a nearly perfect gray circle
Permeated with three jagged holes
Connected by a thin red filament,
I pick up this stone instead.

Descending this slow grassy hill,
I anticipate my daughter's joy
At discovering a whorled beauty,
Suddenly oversized, in her grip.
But this stone resting on my palm
Is unbeautiful, a lump of gravel
To test even a child's sensitivity,
Inspiring only gray indifference.

What story could I tell my daughter
To spark interest in this stone?
That it was once a mountain
Encircled with rings of evergreens
And through forces of erosion
Is small and puckered as a walnut?
Possibly place her finger on a vein
And tell her to feel for a pulse?

Tell her this stone is a tiny casket
With stiffening body curled inside
Whose spirit escapes into air
When chucked against a wall?
Or that this stone preserved my life
Walking toward her in a wind gust,
Its slight weight just enough
To keep my body from stuttering away?

Holding out her hand as I draw near,
My daughter clamps her eyes tight,

Picturing a whorled red flint chip
Or jagged diamond of pink quartzite.
This is a burnt piece of a star
Fallen ten million miles to reach you,
I tell her as I bludgeon her hopes
And slip into her hand this stone.

LONG LIVE ROCK!

The radio blasts Zeppelin's "When the Levee Breaks,"
And the whole quarry's rocking, from the pebble
Approximating the duck walk across one speaker
To the opposite wall, with its blistering feedback.
Lunch hour! Kick out the jams! Crank the amps!

"Led Zeppelin pounds the granite inside my head!"
I yell, losing my footing and nearly careening
Head first down the gravel pile. Drum solo please!
(This quarry loves drum solos! Earnest, energetic,
but inflated solos. Interminable drum variations.)

Leaning way back, Stone Boy ogles the landscape,
The curvaceous groupie lying beyond the chasm,
Only pretending to be absorbed in song,
Two D-sized hills for breasts, the winding road
One seductively arched leg. She wants you, man!

Popping aspirin, Gargoyle's the ultimate cool.
Blank expression, except a blast-mangled lip.
His perpetual tour has marked its fiftieth year,
And now he parties eyes-closed, such a veteran
The best riffs, the best jams, are in his head.

The arena's so packed, it's practically a festival,
Wave upon waves of fans camped out in the rocks,
So many species comprising a virtual love fest.
To say they're mellow would be an understatement.
So fixed in the groove, they're never coming back.

Hey, Robert Plant is starting to sing the blues
(or else he's got gravel stuck in his throat).
I thought you changed batteries in that thing.
Plant's digging deep, the roots of rock and roll.
He's so far down, he's practically underground.

Are we witnessing the death of rock? Or a groove
Only stones can dig. I'm getting sad, man,

Like maybe it's almost time to go back to work.
But not yet. Not before I try out this new riff.
It's only fair. So I lie back and turn to stone.

THE HARD-BOILED PALEONTOLOGIST

God, she was lovely,
Staring into the sky
And floating like a dream.
The kind of bone structure
Guys in my trade flip for,
That's brought stronger Joes
Than me to their knees
For glimpse of an ankle,
Caress of a shoulder.
A heartbreaker for the ages.
She couldn't be more beautiful
If she were alive.

A clean swift job.
Professional hit.
You'd think she was asleep,
Sunning herself on the rocks
Oblivious to all
But for the thoughts
Dancing in her cranium.
I've seen a lot of this
In my line of work,
And perhaps I'm jaded
But this one cut deep,
Like a saber cat tooth.

I grabbed my thermos
And drank it straight,
Steady as a boulder.
This doll had moxie,
I told myself,
Picturing her on a stroll
Out for a bit of air
Or a bite to eat,
In the wrong place
At the right time.
Dead—that's a word
Often used in my trade.

A typical hood, no doubt,
Checks the routine,
Ingratiates himself
Before delivering the proverbial
Cumquat to the brain.
Left her stretched out
As insignificant as gravel
On a dead-end road.
Instinctively, I fingered
The chisel on my belt,
And its best friends,
Pick and hammer.

My brain needed room.
I fired up the jeep
And headed for the office,
Across a landscape
As dry as burnt toast.
Why was I hung up
On this rock-stiff dame,
Just another bone sack
On a granite slab?
Was I somehow seeing myself,
Bounced on a bad hit
With none to mourn my loss?

Another scribbled page
From the book of stones,
A volume thick enough
For several lifetimes
Of sleepless nights,
One I've perused
Many a lonely afternoon,
While a blast-furnace wind
Ruffled its heavy leaves,
All inscribed in code.
Life's a mystery.
You live, you die.

Back in my posh office,
A beat-up trailer
Rocking in the wind,

I watched a cockroach
Jaywalk across the desk
And wished him luck,
Luck in reaching the wall
And especially out there,
Motioning to the rocks
Scattered like marbles
On an endless beach.
Sayonara, little bugger.

When the phone rang,
It was Blackie, my assistant,
With a bombshell:
A second body discovered
Two hundred yards away.
And I got the chills.
This thing was bigger
Than one unlucky dame,
Bigger than me.
I'm talking corruption
Centuries old,
A massive cover-up.

Some Glen or Glenda
Has something to hide
But good.
The type of psycho
Who wants everyone dead
And has the guts.
Who's smooth as quartz
At stashing bodies,
But not above a slip,
And that's where Joes
Like me come in,
Shivs in his side.

EVERYTHING IS A FOSSIL

Exhausted,
I work over the last of the fossils
We gathered this afternoon,
Digging in ravines near the spillway.
Lit only by a small lamp,
The table is covered with tools of the collector:
Brushes, knives, labels, the solution of white glue
Diluted with water
Used to preserve broken fossils
Or to bring out
The delicate quality of the dendrites,
Or the finger-like
Network of veins of angiosperms.
Each specimen is placed, no matter how small,
Into its own carefully marked box or bag,
Or in the small green filing cabinet
In the corner of the room.

My eyes blur.

As I bend over the last find,
The desk becomes its own landscape,
Strewn with boulders, and shells
Of dead life forms begin to move
Across the dark rocks.
My hand is no longer my own,
So still and rigid,
As if it were the hand of someone else,
Or had turned to stone.

Cricket songs wake me up,
So I turn on the light,
Searching at the rug's edge,
Behind the desk,
Until I find it among the rocks,
Resting on a shale piece,
Silent, nearly invisible.

It had crawled there
To get out of the cold.
Its legs barely move when I tap it
With my fingertips, the hard casing
Of its body nearly as firm as stone.
It does not crawl away, hides
Under the shadows of the desk,
So I turn out the light,
And hear nothing the rest of the night.

I find it in the morning,
Legs drawn up, stiff,
And so attached to stone
They break when I lift its fragile form,
Carry it downstairs,
Drop it into the mulch
Around the flowers.
Its body will never survive,
Nor its imprint, nor ours,
But atoms will strike out,
Spinning in ever widening circles,
And be drawn up into other bodies,
Through flowers, the dark stems,
Air's breath.

II. GHOST TOWN ALMANAC

CORPS OF DISCOVERY

Climbing across the bluffs we know how to lose
Our footing and fall to our deaths in the river below.

At night, snuffing out fires to avoid predators,
We feel the jagged edge of the panther's tooth.

Looking up to find we are alone in the dense grass,
We know Adam's terror sweat as he awoke from sleep.

Pulling off our boots around the fire and popping boils,
We step inside the grave and smell the rot.

In dreams, our legs and arms become snakes
That bite us that we may distrust our own bodies.

Weighted by packs and bent double by cramps,
We drop into swamp that we may know humility.

Writing entries by firelight, I let the gray spider live
As it crawls across my pages to prove my humanity.

THE FOUNDER OF OUR TOWN

Five years before the first house, this site was first
inhabited
By a white man on a moonless December night in 1855.
A skirmish between pro-slavery and free-state militiamen
Had occurred ten miles away in a clearing on Sandusky
Creek.
Ten free-staters, led by Josh Douglas, attacked two homes,
Armed with machetes and rifles, dragging off into thick
brush
One father who pleaded with them to spare his life,
Since he had a sick wife and two children not yet ten years.
He was not an active pro-slaver, he swore, only a man
who refused
To take sides, and thus by their definition only, an
enemy of freedom.
He was dressed in worn trousers and shirt; his boots still
rested
Beneath the table he had fashioned out of boards from an
old shed.
All through the trees, he heard his wife screaming,
Begging for mercy, and his youngest, a three-month old
infant,
Wailing like his father's old sow when its throat had been
cut.
Soon he was made to stand up and march into a ravine.
His hands were tied behind his back and he was pushed
face first
Onto the rocks, while a discussion ensued about his fate.
Filled with dread, he thought of his oldest, twelve-year-old
Fred,
Who had been walking to the creek for water when
horses reined in
Outside the cabin, followed by hammerings on the door.
Before he could fetch his rifle, the door burst open, and a
man's face,
The only one he could now remember, had appeared in
the light:
Gray eyes sunken in dark circles, as if a result of
deprivation,

Pitted cheeks and brow, the rest masked by a thick
unkempt beard.
He remembered the high cracking voice, "you are our
prisoner,"
That now silenced all opposition with a single word: "War."
Three free-staters fell on the downed man with broadswords,
Who raised his arms to shield himself from the slashing
blades.
In moments the man lay in the ravine with gashes on
his forehead
And both arms cut away. To make certain, Douglas shot
him in the neck.
"The night's work has been accomplished, and slavery
avenged,"
he shouted, before as agreed upon, the band of men
dispersed,
each in different directions. Douglas rode hard through
thick brush,
stopping finally to rest the horse at this spot, the sight of
our town.
With the horse secured, he huddled all night against a
cottonwood,
Pulling the long coat around him as a northeast storm
commenced,
Raindrops like daggers on his skin.
In the morning, hungry and feverish but reluctant to
start a fire,
He penned a letter to his mother back in Schnectady,
New York:
"God has blessed us here in Kansas, and victories abound.
Though I have fallen in with a band of committed brothers,
This morning I find myself temporarily alone and in ill
health.
This spot, with broad trees and rolling hills,
Reminds me of the land back home which I love so dearly,
Almost more than life itself. A place where after this conflict,
A man could start a fine community, where inhabitants
could
Live as they should—free of chains, violence, and
bitterness."
Having finished the letter, Douglas placed it in his coat
pocket
Between the pages of his Bible,
Raised himself stiffly onto his mount, and rode into history.

REPORT FROM THE BATTLE

"Soldiers in both armies played the game,
whenever and wherever they could,
'just like boys,' one of them remembered."

Geoffrey C. Ward, *Baseball, An Illustrated History*

Bases are expeditiously positioned across the field,
Three soldierless coats and a knapsack for home.
Choosing sides, we name two teams, West and East,
And establish boundaries: two oaks the foul lines,
And for the home run mark the shallow-dug ravine
Where only lately concluded, more dead were buried.

For both sides, two privates were deemed captains,
Advanced in rank by the quickness of their throws,
The facility of their hands, their killer instinct
Which is, at heart, merely a school-boy's ardor.

The West takes the field, expecting a short recess,
Lining their muskets in the grass for easy access.
Joe Puttnam, their catcher, swings his like a bat,
Launching a perfect ball, he says to all, past center,
Tracing it with his eyes into the Confederate camp
And cringing, as everyone laughs, when it explodes.

Taking the outfield, pummeling his fist in his hand,
Runs Jack Chapman, so adept at bringing down flies
He's called, in the game, "death to flying things."
To the bottom of the fourth the game is scoreless.
Murphy's pitching, and two outs down, faces Miller,
Who lowers his shoulder, rockets a blur to center.

Chapman, going back, raises his arm above his head
When there comes a scattering fire from the north
Of which the three outfielders barehand the brunt.
The left and right revive, but the center is lost,
And fallen near the ravine, will not return home.

Miller is the luckiest, we think, whose certain out
Drops harmlessly onto the burnt grass, a home run.

THE BIRTH OF A TEMPORARY TOWN

Only ten days old, and already structures are going up!
At first a rutted path through town, fronting the track.

Choked with refuse—broken chairs, fliers rolling end over end.
Wagons line up on either side; tents bloom like flowers.

Already five mutts have joined together into a pack,
teasing calves tied to stakes, taking down one that strayed.

One girl was bitten from reaching out to pet her former friend.
A blacksmith has set up shop in four crude walls with canvas roof.

From the back of her wagon, an old woman dispenses herbs
to cure gout, drive away bedbugs, and repel rattlesnakes.

Two nights ago, two sixteen year old slatterns defied their fathers
by staying gone all night, returning with bruises and fistfuls of cash.

The first murder has been anticipated for days, as the resident tough
who cheated at cards was beaten by the leader of the prayer service.

"We will not allow drunkenness and dishonesty in our community,"
he repeats, though the prayer service now meets in another's tent.

Already two women in gingham skirts warn their children against
wandering too far down Front Street, down among "those people."

Among endless optimism, one cynic mutters beneath his
breath,
"At rainbow's end, maybe there's just another storm."

SUNDAY MORNING ON MAIN STREET

Hays, Kansas. 1887.

None in town hurries, though it is almost seven o'clock.
Grasping his broom, the gaunt barber stabs at the dirt
Before his shop, and doesn't even glance down the street.
His duel with the wind continues, with the usual result.

Joseph McCoy, the blacksmith, head pounding from
 hangover,
Trips on a horse pile and falls prostrate before the window,
Slicing his hand on broken glass. "Could I have been
 involved?"
His look seems to say, before he stumbles up and on his
 way.
Even with blurred vision, he spots the two women in blue,
The curves of their dresses, and satin bows in their hair.
Conversing before the dry goods store, they set their jaws
In disapproval, turning away with shoulders squared.
Heads forward, they pass the saloon without a word.

By noon no one comes to claim them, and none to bury.
Only the north wind has made an effort, stirring a
 powdery mix
Of dirt and dung to transform the black coats to gray,
And to cover the staring eyes with lids of smithy ash.

The men of town will not return until dark,
Cutting ice blocks from Pipe Creek for summer use.
It is the barber, snipping away at old man Stadler's hair,
Who notices the little red-haired girl in gingham,
Staring hollow-eyed around the corner of the saloon.

Moving to the window with clippers frozen,
Suddenly awakened as if from a day-long sleep,
The barber says to Stadler, "Someone should bury them,
Or move them, so that children won't have to see."
He remembers his first sight of death, a dead horse

Floating down Pipe Creek after an August flood,
How it swirled pinwheel-like in the swift current of his
dreams.

"We should cover them up," he tells a sleeping Stadler,
and even begins to move toward the door
when he watches with relief as the girl steps
around the larger of the two cowboys killed in the brawl,
tripping on this boot, looks down to find blood on her hand,
but only wipes it on her dress and walks on, skips even.

BLACK SHEEP

I'm here to bring
His body home.
Do you have a blanket
Or tarp to cover him up?

I should have thought of it
When I set out two days back.
Zack rode out special
To say he was seen in Abilene.

How long has he been
Strapped to that board
In front of the general store
Without shirt or boots?

The world is a much colder place
That even I could imagine
When children make a game
Of counting wounds.

I'll not bring him home
To Mother this way,
Her arms folded at her chest,
Crowing, "What's he done now?"

Who can explain evil?
Water in the creek
Just follows the course
It sees before it.

My brother killed six men,
Two with a knife,
And wounded six more.
Three had children, I'm told.

No, I'll bury him along the way,
Maybe on that high ridge

Overgrown with weeds
Beyond the creek,

Somewhere that suits him
Where none will remember,
With the sweep of grass
And a pale blue sky,

Where even the brother
Of one he killed
Could stop to rest
In the shade of oaks,

Just for a moment,
Gripping a loaded gun,
Consumed by anger
At all he's lost,

But then stretch out in grass
And close his eyes and maybe
For the first time in a long time,
Forget my brother.

CHADWELL, MILLER, AND PITTS

Northfield, Minnesota. 1876.

The three sit stiffly like penitent schoolboys.
Facing the photographer, they accept their fates,
And if possible, would petition only for shirts
To cover their wounds, or help fend off the cold.

Chadwell sheepishly keeps hands crossed on his lap,
Balled into fists as if dumbly gripping the air,
Or perhaps, in his shame, still fingering the gun.
Chin raised slightly, he concentrates on the wall,
And will not be deterred, no matter how many stare.

Miller remains the most intractable, weakening
Minute by minute, but still struggling with pride.
(Encouraging him, the photographer lowers his head,
crosses his bony hands, and nearly closes his eyes.)
At the next look, Miller's had a change of heart,
Still playing the tough guy but convincing no one,
Eyes bloodshot and swollen and already welling up.

Pitts' smartly combed hair, mustache, and beard,
His resolute jaw, the chiseled bones of his face,
Seem to indicate quality, a distinct gentleman,
Incapable of the wrongs for which he was expelled.
Head inclined forward, glazed eyes staring ahead.
On impulse, the photographer downturns his mouth,
Providing enough remorse even for the Methodists,
And before anyone backslides, snaps the picture.

JACKRABBIT DRIVE

Protection, Kansas. 1910.

An occasional snowflake curls about the frozen fields
Of Jacob Arthur's farm at dawn on New Year's Day,
As the gathering of men, forty-nine strong, mostly farmers,
Drink coffee and chat about the scourge of jackrabbits—
The speed with which they multiply, until desperate for
food,
Entire barns are stripped of feed, and wheat crops destroyed.
Jacob sports his father's Civil War musket, that stormed
The fields of Chancellorsville, vanquishing six Johnny Rebs.
Albin Longron, centerfielder of the town baseball team,
Removes his homemade bats from bag, sixteen in all,
And practices his swing, as easy and natural as at the plate.
Despite the ribbing and easy banter, we never forget
This is cold calculation designed to secure our way of life,
Something more than a game that stirs winter blood,
Competitive spirit, and scorn from our womenfolk.
Finally, Jacob fires "Old Blue" as a signal to begin,
And the forty-nine drivers fan out across stubble fields
In two groups led by Hugh Prather and J. P. Caudill,
Unleashing the dogs which race ahead into the brush.
The black-tailed jackrabbit can spring five feet in one leap,
Even with a body emaciated from winter starvation,
And this seems to quell the feeling this is mass slaughter,
Rather than a contest between opponents on a level plain—
Speed and numbers as a match for our guns, bats, and dogs.
As we tread over frozen earth, we continually test our aim,
More to move the herd forward than to thin the ranks.
Ten boys with gunny sacks walk behind the lines of men,
Grabbing carcasses by the long ears and heaving them in,
Wishing they were old enough to sport ten-gauge shotguns
And banter as easily as men above the continuous reports:
"Jacob, even if that were Johnny Reb instead of a jackrabbit,
he'd have been in Alabama before your ball left the barrel!"
The boys begin complaining about the weight of the sacks,
Though before us, driven by dogs, several hundred
jackrabbits

Head for the first line of pens constructed of chicken wire.
There this endeavor, one of taunts and superior marksmanship,
Becomes no longer game or sport, but life and death struggle,
As the gates of the pens are closed, trapping them inside.
With two other men, Albin walks among the leaping mass,
Showing off that famous home run swing time after time.

LAND OF THE POST ROCK

Backed by a line of stone posts strung with wire,
Roughly chiseled and leaning at various angles,
The old man standing in the vine-carpeted field
Seems merely a stray too stubborn to follow orders,
A post hopelessly off track with the plodding march
Wandering inch by inch into a watermelon patch,
Equally bent, with the same scarred discolored face
Notched in odd striations as if by hammer blows.
The puzzled look on his face expresses surprise
At the distance he has traveled without realizing,
As if his thoughts had only momentarily drifted
And suddenly he has awakened to a new position
Tangled with vines in a field of round stones.
His left hand grasps his hat, the right balances
On its fingers a quarter-moon watermelon rind
Turned slightly upward toward the old man's face,
Held as if it were producing a sound, a low hum
Or dull ring such as stone makes when broken.
The ground around him is littered with stones,
Covering as if rained down from the gray sky.
And the old man gazes out at the photographer,
Inquiring how, in a land of nothing but stone,
The skies could open up only to deliver more.

BLUEGRASS TILL DAWN

The founder of bluegrass
Wears an ill-fitting pork pie hat,
And abuses his unattractive wife,
Tying her to the bed,
Telling her it was all her fault.

The ill-constructed cabin
Overlooking the creek
Is a sieve to winter winds,
Draining away his will,
Leaving only kernels of hate.

Just before sunset,
Diphtheria killed the child,
Who played in the corner
Building log cabins
Out of corn cobs.

The cabin is dark,
Save for embers,
And wind screams
Through wall cracks,
Echoing in the dead grass.

All night he plays the fiddle,
A gift from his father
Three hundred miles away,
Above the wife's moans
And rustling of bluegrass.

THE BLIZZARD OF 1888

Jonathan slips away
When the teacher
Turns to the board,
Putting his shoulders to the door
With a hard shove to get away,
Always her "little fighter,"
Kicking out at the walls
When he is reprimanded
As if to remind her who he is,
And she, because she loves him
Despite his rambunctious spirit,
Will quiet him with a tender pat
And word of endearment
That she knows he can hear
Though he will only shrug away
And kick out at her again.
Now with a shout, she spots him
Slipping away beneath the gray sky
Widening and stretching with a storm,
First his oblong matted head
Poking from the thick brush,
Then the squirming plump body
Squirting across the meadow
Already a thin snowy sheet.
That night, before the hearth,
His mother watching with relief,
He stretches his fingers and toes
Before the warmth and sighs
Oblivious to the miracle of life.

In the schoolhouse,
The children grow silent,
And even the teacher's hand
Freezes before the blackboard
When the room grows dark,
And all look around blankly
When a woman's cry echoes

Down through the stovepipe
And beneath the door crack.
But the teacher knows the signs
Of an impending blizzard.
Clutching her midsection
As if seized by hard cramps,
She pulls them close
Around her in the cloakroom,
For she loves them though
She's only held them so long,
These children she'll never have.
Even into the howling night,
When the firewood runs out
And their fingers turn blue,
she holds them close.

But it is Samuel's name
She calls, over and over,
When the children grow quiet
And the howl of her conscience
Tugs at the chinks in the wood.
She can no longer remember
The offense, as if that matters now,
That caused her to grab his back
And push him through the door,
To set him out along the river home
With a note that read "Expelled."
She can only imagine him now
Blinded by the sudden white sheet,
Grabbed by long icy fingers,
And with a tight fierce grasp
Not without a merciful quickness,
Strangled to fall back pale and limp.
"Samuel, Samuel," the teacher cries,
Still murmuring this two days later
When her husband opens the door
And holds her in his arms.

THREE VERSIONS OF CAP EVANS' POOL HALL

Marion, Kansas. 1904.

The first is sketchy, zeroing in on the angles
Of the narrow building, looking from the extreme
Right front corner, diagonally to opposite left.
The line of four pool tables, like a knifeblade,
Slices the floor in half, ceiling beams parallel
To the crouching tables, as if in collusion,
Gathering in close proximity at the back wall
Above the still door, with the explosive energy
Of discordant creatures unnaturally confined.
Above each table, a lantern dangles by a wire,
Like a spider lowering itself upon its prey,
Filament upon filament, just inches at a time.
The left wall is bare, save for a rack of cues,
And an indecipherable sign, its block letters
Unaccountably blurred, poised as if containing
A last word on why the hall is so oddly empty,
Its atmosphere seemingly drawn up so tight
Even an echo couldn't travel but a few feet.
Why the tables crouch like wounded animals,
The room itself twisted with expectation,
Back door under pressure of an enormous wind.

The four men occupying the hall in the second
Look as if simultaneously aware of the sting
Of decay rising from the discolored carpet,
Mildew rippling out toward the hall's corners,
Just reaching the feet of the closest player,
Who tenses as he discerns its clammy grip.
The two pairs seem oblivious to each other,
Separated by gulfs of age and knowledge,
Though all project a laborer's weariness,
All now looking toward the front of the hall,
As if someone they've dreaded has arrived,
Perhaps the foreman who daily terrorizes

With shouted curse word or slap of a fist,
His hobbled footsteps across the concrete
Unmistakable in the dim echoes of the shop,
His bitter breath putrefying in the heat.
The players seem shocked at his showing,
The casual arrogance such a move betrays,
Determining his presence like the mildew
In the air, with burning of nostrils.

The youth pretending manhood in the third
Pose on opposite ends of the second table,
Their anonymity shielded by the dim lantern
As if their presence is a security breach
(deftly slipping by the sleeping proprietor,)
as if any moment the working men would return
to sweep them like dust back in the street.
As if expecting it, they wear caps and coats,
Nervously absorbed in the game, or pretending,
One with his back turned away from the door,
The other bent but only to gauge his shot,
Yet with his bony back tensed like a spring,
Set to fly him in fear through the back door
Into the void of the alley, and his youth.
The sign on the wall, now clearly legible,
Looms up in stark detail, “Pay As You Go,”
Though they’ve not yet begun to understand
The distance they’ll be required to travel,
Fighting the twin urges to run and stay
Even as loud voices sound in the street
And the fat proprietor awakens from sleep.

HOPI MAIDEN WITH SQUASH BLOSSOM HAIRDRESS

Awaiting the moment, she lowers her left shoulder,
Squares neck and forehead, as the photographer
Edges her with his camera lens to the adobe wall,
Unnervingly patient, refusing to trip the shutter.

Her body, even hands, hidden by ceremonial dress,
He zeroes in on her face, broad focused eyes
Acknowledging no shame, revealing no concessions,
Not even to lower, narrow the corners, or blink.
Her determined mouth and jaw, angular cheekbones,
Weakening, might have to surrender momentarily
To break a bitter smile, as if lowering a weapon.
Twisted into whirling squash blossoms, her hair
Unravels, bows in simple strands, and reconvenes.
Only the birth mark, a tiny cactus, above her nose
Remains constant, like a fossil embedded in stone.

Stubborn, the photographer scrutinizes the face,
Examining eyelashes brittle as if fire-scorched,
Waiting for a slight lowering to signal the end.

At a draw, but gaining, the photographer slips,
Sliding his sweating finger across the switch,
Capturing the girl almost at her breaking point.
Defiant, the grim traces of a smile on her lips,
Fervent brow curled at the edges, nothing more.

PRAIRIE PHANTOM

Trails the wagon
West from Kansas City,
Cracking wheel spokes
And splintering axles.

Sits beside the man
On the wagon seat,
Repeating, "Only a failure
Would journey here."

Pulls the covers
From the infant boy
On a cold night,
Bringing pneumonia and death.

Whispers in the ear
Of the thin woman
Digging his grave,
"Join him."

MENTAL NOTES OF A KANSAS HERMIT

Walk through bramble and get stung by a wasp to see
One blue wildflower burning in a red meadow.

Fly a kite constructed of reeds and newsprint,
Or weighted by stones, build a fortress for ants.

Tear down the snow fence, but save the posts.
Walk through time, but always return before dusk.

Eat a hatful of berries with two wild onions
And wash your breath with a tin cup of rain.

Deny the existence of prairie phantoms
When they snuff out kindling or watch you sleep.

Owe allegiance to things you can touch,
Dirt and wood, to replace God, country, wind.

Send a fifth bottle down the swollen creek
With a note inside that reads "Be my friend."

THE DAY I BECAME AN EXILE

This is the story—
That I was driven from town
By an angry mob

Armed with pitchforks,
Torches raised,
Rousing house after house

To check behind woodpiles,
Stabbing hay in barn lofts
With pitchfork prongs.

Intimidating my distant cousin
Who hadn't spoken to me in years
By backing him to the stove,

They suggested I was hidden
Beneath a rug-covered trapdoor
Or stretched out on attic beams,

Then waited for me to sneeze
Or arms aching, let a knee fall
Onto a creaking two-by-four.

My cousin who barely knew me
Took an elbow in the neck
As the vigilantes grew desperate,

While minutes ahead of the dogs,
I lowered myself into the creek
Despite my hatred of leeches.

Hollow reed between my lips,
I breathed in the thin August heat
Until the murmurs passed,

Then eluded those with the noose,
Slept in piles of dead leaves while
Heading due north to upcountry.

As the story goes, I lived in my cabin
With an eye for sudden movement,
Fearful of telltale smoke trails.

In truth, the day I left town
Only a mongrel dog acknowledged
My silent walk by lifting one ear.

Only one paintless shutter opened
As I passed the last row of houses
And turned into the quiet grass.

I built this sod cabin over months
And lifted my eyes toward town
Only to note a soaring hawk or heron

Gliding down to observe my labors.
I lived without care or worry,
An exile by indifference.

BARKER

Paola, Kansas. 1926.

Always crisp, freshly combed, impeccably dressed.
Spiritless and implacable, the only exceptional act.
Out-freaking even the bearded lady and Snakewoman
In creepy repose, his seemingly unshakeable faith
In the paunchy young acrobat clambering gingerly
Onto the platform, breathlessly climbing the ladder,
Reaching the mark with only a brief worried glance
And a weary smile to a visibly relieved audience.
Hyperbolically announcing each death-defying feat,
The old barker never looks up, not a wrinkle moves,
Becomes most remarkable then (when his spiel ends),
How he stands coolly unconcerned with the degree
To which the world matches his expectations.
Statuesque, inflexible, the barker stares ahead
At a bare stretch of ground just past the crowd
As the acrobat, wiping sweat, prepares to leap.

Though never applauded, the barker's on display,
A slender mummy raised from the Valley of Kings,
Impeccably preserved, drained of all imperfections.
Not the king, but his long-suffering manservant,
Eternally glossing over the young royal's mistakes,
Praising him for the smallest of accomplishments,
Shrouding his own boredom, and superiority over all.

GHOST TOWN ALMANAC

January

Another year of survival!
You're strong, determined,
But possess no illusions.
Maintaining any presence,
Even a rock or rotting board,
Is a lofty goal at this date.
Don't catalogue your losses,
A list stretching to December.
In the stages of grief,
Resignation replaces fury,
And peace supplants resignation.
A deep snow late on the twentieth
Effects a mild depression.
Think of it as lock and key
Preventing additional theft.
Conserve limited energy.

February

Courage will be tested
By this bitter short month.
But courage is overrated.
Call it a lack of desperation
At facing the inevitable.
Anyone can manage that.
This is not a suitable month
For earnest rumination,
The mind tracking away
Through snowdrifts despite the cold.
But don't shun the past,
The immense hulk
Beneath the iceberg's tip.
Memories of blazing hearths,
Punchlines of caustic jokes,
And kettles of steaming beans.

March

Expect highs and lows.
Spring thaw begins
On a sunny fifteenth.
A time of celebration
Accompanied by a measure of grief.
Melting snow, runoff, and rain
Produce additional erosion.
The protruding edge of the well pump
Disappears beneath sediment.
The bank's buried cornerstone
Sinks two more inches.
But some old friends return!
The top half of a whisky bottle
And a rust-eaten metal shaft
Materializing out of red clay.
Catch up on old times.

April

The cruelest month.
For one of your sensitivity
And brooding melancholy,
A period of loneliness
Unchecked by wildflowers
Sprouting at the edges of rocks
And sprigs of roses.
The rise of new life
At the corners of your world
Supplies only false companionship,
Slender figures and sunny faces
Without character or grace.
Such are your enemies
Bent on your destruction,
Undertakers in colored shirts
Looking down and smiling.

May

The rigidity of winter
Segues into summer's ease.
You will meet a dark stranger
With knapsack and camouflage hat
Around noon on the fifth,
Stirring echoes of the past.
Something about gesture or stance.
Could he be the fresh start
The wind always promised?
The second coming?
Or just a wandering hiker
Who neglects to acknowledge you.
Or worse, fails to notice you.
Choose the latter now
And avoid disappointment.
Learn to love yourself.

June

Lingering haze.
A flood on the seventh
Bathes you in broken limbs,
Aluminum cans, and sludge.
But little washes away
Except a measure of pride.
Pride is a privilege
Best left to populated cities.
Near the end,
Priorities are rearranged,
Survival and dignity first.
Endurance. Lack of bitterness.
A day, even week, of hopelessness
Is natural in your situation.
Occasional panic attacks.
No advice can soften them.

July

An independent spirit
Has served you well.
Living on your own terms.
Isolation is one side effect
Of an independent spirit.
The betrayal of loved ones
In the face of loyalty
Tears at the mortal coil.
On Independence Day,
You will ironically feel dependent
On those who once gave you life,
Who carved you from the plains,
Whose laughter shook the air,
And silence seeped into the rocks.
They made life worth living.
Toast them with a cup of air.

August

The lack of groundwater
The second half of the month
Turns the mind inward,
Searching for old wells
With dark smoky water
Tasting of iron and fire.
You are multi-dimensional
With a wealth of inner resources,
An ability to look below the surface,
A fondness for late afternoon sky,
An abiding love for level ground.
You've developed an appreciation
For things previously ignored
In the wealth of abundant life:
The slow arch of a falling leaf
Onto what was once Main Street.

September

The fall intensely beautiful,
So prepare for depression.
The rush of wind will sadden you,
Grasshoppers will annoy you.
An echo of school bells
From some immeasurable cavern
Inside an aluminum pop can
Inspires five days' reflection
On all you've learned
In one hundred forty years.
Your memory suffers from age,
Complicated by depression.
Even your name comes and goes,
Unspoken for eighty-five years.
You quickly become distraught.
End of reflection.

October

The stripping of undergrowth,
Peeling away the nonessential
To reveal one version of the truth,
Begins with an early frost
Occurring on the fifteenth,
Full moon, no clouds.
Assessment requires a cold eye,
A head prepared for the worst,
The eschewing of romantic spirit
Unless results are unsatisfactory.
Sometimes truth needs a mask,
Dark figure hidden by costume,
A fatal trap disguised by leaves.
A season of expectation,
Of hoping for the best.
Good luck.

November

Trees stripped and skeletal,
Ravishing in silhouette.
A late autumn version of beauty
After eighty intervening years
You can now apply to yourself,
To fossil-encrusted gapped foundations,
Wheel ruts of forgotten streets,
Children's breath frozen in air,
The slanting spare landscape
Eloquent with understatement,
As the sun slips from the sky
Like a deadbeat tenant owing rent,
And vows never to return.
It will return.
Cultivate a sense of grace
And a thankful spirit.

December

Another year concludes,
A victory of sorts.
A good measure of soaking rain
Reaching your deepest roots
But only a dusting of snow,
Like showers of cottonwood down,
Late on the twenty-first.
In the clear crisp frigid air,
It remains through the thirty-first,
A good steady companion
To ease you into another year
Spirited for winter sleep.
Appreciate the wealth of life
Occurring at the end when it comes.
For now offer a heartfelt toast
To good friends, snow and wind.

III. HAPPY HOUR AT VERA'S

INTRO

There is an area
You may know
In this world
So quiet,

Things stir
Only from the safety
Of being underneath.

This is the land
Where I was born.

RAISINS

Forty miles southwest of Newton, Kansas,
Will Danham grew grapes on the side of a hill.

Eating some, and
Selling the rest to make wine.

When he moved there twenty years ago he told
Mr. Mauley the banker
That he wanted to plant

Little green balls that looked like marbles
And he wouldn't need a truck for he would merely
Roll them down the hill into town
Sort of like a roundup (only down).

The neighbors, corn-fed, whole-wheated
Till the stalk grew from their ears
Shook their heads in amazement
And chaff flew off like dandruff.

Will Danham became something of a joke,
As you can imagine,
Especially to farmers on Saturday morning,
And the secretary at the local cooperative
Who always told him "good day"
When he asked for spray.

Before she died, Mrs. Danham (his wife) swore
Repeatedly that nothing could ever
Make her forgive him for the embarrassment
And gave birth to seven children
To remind him of it when she was gone.

Years and years and grapes still grew on the hill
Overlooking Bull Creek where Danham lived.

Eating more and more, and
Selling even less to make wine.

He supposed it must have been their roundness
That intrigued him, lines upon lines
Drawing in upon themselves to make cycles.

Driving his tractor back and forth
Pulling the small crowded furrows from under
The earth till grape vines stood
In neat little rows,
He could see this was so—cycles.

It was in mid-April, when the first beginnings
Of grapes appeared on the vines,

Will Danham went gray;
All of a sudden he felt the contraction,
The easing,
The slow rhythmic pressure on the chest,
Crawling on hands and knees
Up to the porch,

And resting there
For the rest of the summer watching
The careless restless movings of the farm.

The rows,
Divided neatly into squares,
Became jagged and worn.

Rains came,
Fall,
And leaves blew across his path.

The grapes, round,
Smooth-skinned and juicy,
Like tiny hearts,
Around mid summer grew ripe,
Reddened, and fell to the ground.

They lay in the sun,
But he had raisins.

HAPPY HOUR AT VERA'S

Hunter, Kansas.

"On the wings of a snow-white dove,
He sends his pure sweet love..."

Less like a dove than a spindly underfed hen,
Vera maneuvers among graffiti-laden tables
Snatching up glasses with the quick motion
Of a chicken pecking corn, discerning empties
Like scattered grains among tall grass,
No hesitation or wasted motion, all smiles.
For this is Happy Hour, the hall is crowded,
Vera is dressed to kill, with polyester slacks,
A tee-shirt with her round face on the front
And written underneath, "Vera's—Hunter, Kansas."

Already sweat beads on her lip's velvety down,
A widening water pool gathers at each armpit.
And on her way she's telling a familiar tale,
In her tremulous squawk, of the night Willie
Crashed his car into the pool hall's west side,
Sending glasses and pool balls flying outward,
And of how she chased him down Victor Street
Till he fell in a blind stagger at her feet
Begging, "Be merciful, O great vengeful bird,
Most vicious buzzard, and fly to your cave."

Vera finishes up, and everyone toasts Willie,
"the only worm to ever ruffle Vera's feathers,"
laughing loudly but with the unsettling image
of a fuzzed-up Vera hovering above their eyes
mistaking them for gravel bits to feed her craw.
As if to dispel the image, Johnson calls out,
"Vera, sing the dove song!" amid loud approval,
though some mumble amiably, "Now you done it."

Vera sets down her tray, immediately obliges
With a song she's sung some thousands of times,

But never on key, filled with occasional honks
And general skimming above and below the tune,
Abruptly ending before once more taking flight,
Putting the exhausted bird through its paces
With the same message held fast in its claws.

Then somebody clips money into the juke box
And sheepishly Willie walks from the corner
To take Vera's hand, pull her to the floor,
Twirl her about in an awkward semi-pirouette,
Then absolved, pass her to the next one,
Vera grasping each as if from some duty,
Carrying him like he was a broken twig,
Setting him down on the opposite hallway
The way a dove culls sticks for a nest.

FISHING ON THE KAW RIVER RULE

One thing you must remember
If you're gonna stand on
The banks of the Kansas River:

Fish, fish, if you will.
Let everyone see you smile
As you try to reel in the big one.
Just don't be too quiet
About it. Though
Nobody wants you to yell.

TIPTOE THROUGH THE TOMBSTONES

In June I turned eight,
Was too small for my big bones,
The year Grandpa grabbed a ukulele
And tiptoed through the tombstones.

Food was scarce, and laughter more.
If started, we might never have quit.
Each meal could be the meal Grandpa
Choked down the last hard biscuit.

Kids at school called me "skeleton,"
Said I rattled in the halls.
After school, I walked in the woods
Where not even Momma could call.

Wind played songs in the grass,
But our house was still down to dark.
Grandpa couldn't walk or speak.
Dying was his art.

He'd worked in a plant for forty years,
Breathing fumes that made him sick.
Momma said sometimes he came home
And couldn't make a fist.

"An old man is trapped inside you,"
my momma said, "trying to get out.
Get your head out of books.
Take hold of now."

If there was an old man inside me,
Maybe he was like Grandpa Jay—
Mouthing words that wouldn't come
And staring into space.

"Each man needs a place in this world,"
Grandpa used to say. "This you'll learn.
Mine kept moving, Kansas to Korea,
Now underground, to fatten worms."

JANUARY TRAIN

The train in January
Slips through unnoticed

Cutting across a field,
Over the frozen creek,

Its horn blast, if sounded,
Muted by falling snow.

If its wheels run on tracks,
They are disguised by drifts.

If the deer glances up
From tufts of dead grass

Does it detect a shadow,
A blur of rusted cars,

The rumble of wheels,
Or nothing at all?

If, in the brick house
Around the bend,

The woman suddenly awakes
To a steady vibration,

Water on the nightstand
Quaking in the glass,

Does she close her eyes
And return to sleep,

Or does she rise
To check her dying father,

His downstairs room
Suddenly free of snores,

Tiptoeing on bare feet
On wooden floors,

Pushing open the door
To find him gone.

DOOMSDAY

You see that plane just breaking the trees
Above Kanapolis, I'm telling my good buddy
Already half-stoned from Double Trouble 7-Up.
It'll circle around town two or three times,
Dive in low just as you're saying your "I do's,"
And drop the bomb that'll end life as you know it.
You'll stagger out from beneath burnt boards,
Wipe fallout from your eyes,
Spot the pilot on the horizon waving his wings,
Without care or thought as to the devastation
Billowing up in a mushroom cloud back there.
Plane in hangar, he'll make a snack,
Kick his feet up on the Captain's cherry oak desk,
And tell dirty jokes to all other pilots
Just back from weddings across the world.
Meanwhile, free from rubble, you'll turn to the town
And won't recognize the place, maybe a building
Or car or blackened sign that points the wrong way,
"40 Miles to Wichita" aimed straight at the sky.
One by one, the rest of the church will stagger out,
Now with blurred faces and bodies
Moving like clouds across manicured grass,
Like zombies brought back from the dead,
Shaking your hand and slapping your back.
And then there's the wife, holding your hand
As if nothing has happened, as if smoke . . .

Okay, I'll shut up. I've been married twice.
Cohabitating ain't what it's cracked up to be,
But I'm not going to stand up in this church
And object to the marriage of my good buddy,
Even if he's the last unattached friend I've got.
I'll just sit in this converted broom closet
That reeks of turpentine, bleach, and feet,
Saying nothing, just me and the cockroaches.

DELMER

As a child he had large hands
Long rickety arms,
A thin mouth that rarely spoke
And eyes like black marbles.

For a boy with so many flaws,
His hands drew all the attention,
Bruised swollen knuckles,
Fingers the width of cigars.

Delmer knew the power of his hands,
Chopping wood or slopping hogs,
Pinching flies between fingers,
Holding girls who tried to run.

At fifteen they were worn and tough,
Loose-skinned like an old man's.
A landscape threaded with ravines
And dirt roads leading nowhere.

Staring at them handcuffed,
After that girl broke his finger
And ran bruised to a nearby farm,
Delmer disappeared into the canyons.

On the outside he worked lumber,
Cattle, anything with his hands.
Gradually gaining some acceptance
Among men for his steady touch.

Some days when the work is slow,
He'll show the boys how to douse.
Grasp a Y-shaped willow branch
And walk it above a water pipe.

Willow branch ahead and pointing up,
Delmer paces the lumber yard alley,

Until it quivers and begins to move,
Plunges forward and points below.

Holding hands out for inspection,
Delmer stares with the rest,
As if they belonged to another,
Or had a mind of their own.

A wart on each thumb and forefinger,
One vein that pulses with his heart,
As if the levee were ready to crack
And flood his wrist with blood.

WANDA'S FRIED CHICKEN

DANCE NIGHT AT THE FONTANA CIVIC CENTER

The song ends, but Joe doesn't know it,
Frail arms and legs still pecking away
Putting a new spin on the Funky Chicken
As danced to forties' big band standards.

Joe may not know when the ax falls,
At least if Death taps his bony shoulder.
May think he's trying to muscle in on his woman,
Her with the mustache and support hose,
Arthritic hands, and labored breath.
"If that's Death, let him get his own chick,"
Joe might say. "Take old Wanda Davis,
Starved like a pullet for fifteen years.
Grab a wrinkled spur or bald wing
And dance a quick rumba to the bone yard,"
He tells Death, catching Wanda's gaze
As she considers throwing him a bone,
Imagining what he would look like naked,
An old plucked rooster
With sagging comb, barely able to cluck,
Let alone crow, and tough to boot.

"Dinnertime," she yells, and the floor clears,
a skyful of hawks swooping in for the kill.
Golden perfection: legs, thighs, and breasts.
Joe eats with an almost cannibalistic glee,
Wanda believes, the ancient cock of the walk,
Walking bandy-legged back to his bloated pullet,
Rhode Island Red with high-pitched cluck.
How many eggs can she lay in one sitting?
Wanda imagines Joe as one of the yardbirds
Squawking and scrambling in her cramped coop,
Flapping his dumb wings to save his life.
Then quickly, to benefit all womankind,
He's undone at the neck, left to flop,
Drained, dressed, singed, soaked, and fried.

But at least he's a rooster, she considers,
And not Jack Spoon, the Great Horned Owl,
Hooting an old jibe to get her attention,
With his cowlick and big round spectacles.
At least Joe could stir up a little dust
In the henhouse, and crow in the new day.

Let them fight it out behind the elevator
With hay bales for stands and pits of straw.
Joe could be the fat end of my wishbone,
Wanda thinks, suddenly catching Joe's gaze
As he admires her delicate shank and wattle,
The way she roosts without a single cackle,
Her eyes like two gravel bits burning
A fiery path to his gizzard and craw.

WIZARD OF WHEELS

Wizard of wheels
Is what we called him in the town,
Near thirty-five, must have been,
Worked long hours for my daddy, and
I knew him many times from when
We'd sprung him out of jail.

He's been working for my daddy most
Of two years come the spring now;
At fixin' cars daddy says he's 'bout
The best to come around
Since Joe T. Johnson way back in my
Grandfather Waters' time.

My momma says he was born for bad,
Gets drunk most every night, and he was
Locked up twice for that,
But I think there's somethin' else myself,
He fixed the tire on my bike the summer last,
Said, "There you go, Cap,"
But nothin' else.

Sometimes I seen him drive out the country
In his red and black Pontiac,
Drive real slow down a mile to the station,
Watch the trains
With a bottle in his hands,
Trains and trouble 'bout all he's seen much of
Since Wizard's been in our town.

Was only days ago he left for good,
Got drunk, hit the sheriff,
Took the long way down to the station in the rain,
And while I's watchin'
Ran alongside one jumped a freight.

Sittin' on the wheel he fixed I watched
The Wizard of Wheels
Ride out of our town for good.

LONG DAY AT MUDDY CREEK

He was a slack-jawed sheepherder,
With a mug like a wrinkled map,
The lonesomest stretch of country
Viewed by beast or man.

His eyes two black boulders
In hollowed-out ravines.
The only visitor an occasional hawk
Checking out the scene.

The flickering of an old memory
Flapping tired wings.
Waiting for the stir of breath,
That smoky croaking wind.

It was the time of the great drive,
A hundred sheep on an eight-day trek,
Across pastureland and Highway 9
To winter range near Muddy Creek.

Braving the speeding semi trucks,
The elements of wind and flurry,
The cowboy shepherd drove his flock
A hundred deep into the prairie.

That drive was a genuine ass-buster
Atop old Bob's sway-backed roan.
"My dancin' days are through,
and my wild seeds are sewn."

No less hard on the sheep.
Twenty ewes died at Muddy Creek
Shortly after delivering lambs,
That long cold winter sleep.

The longest day of his life.
Twenty orphans in his trailer

Bleating for food, food, food,
And couched in Pampers.

It was no fondness for sheep,
No festering of human love,
That kept him changing diapers
With one eye on the stove.

It was a desperate measure
To keep this luxurious trailer,
All the fine things in life,
His coffee pot and blender.

A pan of milk for bottles.
No drop of whisky in sight.
“Put a saddle on the stove, mother,
we’re ridin’ the range tonight.

TRAP

My old man
Traps the south bank of Sand Creek
In a flat-bottomed row boat.
At dawn, lower lip packed with Red Man,
Shoulder strung with blood-flecked traps,
He trolls broken limbs, stumps,
Rank stew-like swamp,
Tripping over frozen deer turds
Back to his hidden places,
Sizing up the beaver or fox
With his bent hickory cane
And smashing its skull
With one fierce quick stroke.

The old son of a bitch
Hit me yesterday
To warn me not to run away again,
And so I slept in the shed
Curled up like a raccoon cub,
Dizzy like the sparrow that
Cracked the kitchen window
And fell back stunned and throbbing.

Meanwhile,
His coyote
Chews up two of his boots
And his leather poncho
And growls when I make a move
For the door. To distract him,
I toss him the old man's wallet.

Sitting on the wood pile,
I can hear him barking,
A mixed-up crazy thing
That would chew off his foot
To break for the woods.

A TOUR OF BLOOM

North of Bloom
Is a lone oil well
That never stops
(pumping nothing
but stale air),
a steel marker
that commemorates
the "Highest Point
in the County,"
another that marks
the lowest point,
two miles away.

South of Bloom,
A converted hearse/
Demolition derby car
Sits on its axle
Filled with beer cans
("250 soldiers
who made the world
a better place").
In the driveway
Of an abandoned farm,
A sign reads
"Beware of Ghost Dog!"

East of Bloom,
A man drives a pickup
With this bumper sticker:
"BLOOM—CORRUPTION
CAPITAL OF THE U.S."
A bullet-shot sign states
"54 Miles to the World's
Largest Ball of Twine,"
And in spray paint
Directly beneath
"1/2 Mile to the World's
Largest Bag of Wind."

West of Bloom
Is a bar with this sign,
"Poor Service, Warm Beer,"
a barn with a target
painted on the roof,
a convenience store
with a postcard
of a topless woman
driving a police car
with the caption,
"Kansas speeders
will be violated!"

RODEO

The cheers of the crowd
Their easy banter
Echoes in silent waves

Across the rodeo arena
Gray and frozen
Under a winter sky.

Last July's extravaganza
Was well-attended
But this crowd is infinite!

Bullish and expectant,
Wind tears
At the chute gates.

Riding the air,
Bucking and rocking,
A snowflake hits the dirt.

In the holding pens,
Leaves skitter
Like nervous colts.

An empty bag
Bloated and brash
Staggers for the exit.

A loose cord
On the ticket booth
Waves more in.

Weeds tick them off,
One at a time,
On a chain-link fence.

No need for tickets
Or hand stamps
Or life.

BURNING THE FIELDS

Flames creep
across the bottoms
like serpents on fire.

Gray smoke jets
with silent engines
race across the Kansas sky.

The ancient farmer,
charred by soot,
paws at the flames

like an wounded black bear,
fork prongs stabbing
just to hear them scream.

ELECTRICITY

Black clouds swell, and burst
With invitation,
As does every Midwestern town,
And in such a contraction
Glen Harding was struck with lightning,
And the flash lit up the town
Of Wellsville, Oklahoma.

Glen, running away the deep intention
Of leaving Wellsville forever,
Was struck while standing
On U.S. Highway 69
With a flattened tire,
And he hadn't got far
From town when it happened.

Wellsville said it served him right,
Leaving a wife and family,
And after he recovered from the shock,
It seems he saw the light,
For he forgot his intentions
And labored on and on in a Wellsville plant,
Thinking he loved his wife
All the while.

But like storm clouds, which contract and return
In the Midwestern skies
Without an invitation,
Memories returned to Glen Harding
Over the years
Of a night spent in a hayloft
With a farm girl
When the harvest was done,

And one rainy evening
In the middle of summer,
Glen Harding vanished in the deepening twilight

Through darkened fields,
And although Mrs. Harding says he'll be back
Like before,
She knows he won't,
For lighting never strikes twice
In the same place.

HOG HEAVEN

Bliss used to come in small short gulps,
The leaking slop buckets the farmer brought
Or late afternoon kicks in the crowded wallow.
But now Heaven seems a much wider place,
Large enough for the greediest appetite.
How can I be satisfied with this trough
When I've seen brothers swallowed in rapture
Vanishing in a crest of fragrant foam?

The world had become a pig's paradise,
A swirling ocean of fermented swill
That drove the old farmer from his home,
And now slowly inched toward our pen,
Twenty yards, fifteen yards, ten yards.
After such a feast, a fattening,
We could lie forever in the muddy sludge,
Free to grunt, squeal, stretch, and snort,
Bellies growling with delicious gas.
"I'm going to drink it all," I squealed,
"down the last little drop, then explode!"

Shaking, I put my forelegs in the trough
And raised my snout to gaze at Heaven.
That's when I saw the farmer's boat
Sweep around the barn and power down,
Avoid the tractor cab, and come to rest
Five yards from the pen. Five yards!
Then he began loading us into the boat,
One by one, but not without a fight.
"He's not taking me alive," I screamed,
as he put his arms around my stomach,
lifted me to his shoulders, and let me drop.
I remember his breath, and his smooth hands
Pinching my side as I briefly struggled,
Tried to kick, and then let myself go.
Let my snout bounce against the seat
And my body quickly sink into resignation.

Fear and shame kept me quiet,
Nuzzling the gray sludge under his boots,
As we motored off in the growing dark,
Waves of Heaven slapping at the sides.
Then the gray shoat began to crack,
Squealing and squirming, not giving in,
The vision we'd all waited for so close,
Just a breath away. Struggling, fighting,
As the man vainly grasped at the hooves
Just at the shoat toppled off the lip,
Broke the surface with a loud squeal,
Then disappeared in a gathering foam,
Free and clear and happy forever.

NO. 102

A flood fades from memory
once high water disappears,
slinking out the front door
and down the muddy road.

This last was no worse
than the others I've endured,
for my foundation is strong,
could last another eighty years.

How easily they dismiss you,
avoid you like a cancer.
Toss hedge-apples at windows,
drive slowly just to stare.

Even the man with red paint
whistled as he approached,
soaked his brush in the can
and slashed numbers on the door.

When the old lady returned
to retrieve her last belongings,
she scurried back to the car
and didn't even close the door.

I apologize for the odor,
bitter mold that burns the nose.
Thick carpet of river sludge,
rotting carpet circling the tub.

But I never turned anyone out
for any bad habit or bent.
The old lady barely kept house,
so she should be used to dirt.

I thought she might understand
what rejection feels like.

No visitors came for months.
Her best friend was daylight.

But no, I'm a grim reminder
of a great human catastrophe,
and so must be expunged,
the sooner the better.

There are still a few items
she needs to retrieve,
a photograph of a child
in stark black and white.

A thin silver necklace
buried in the closet.
She could still find it
with a little luck.

THE GEOGRAPHIC CENTER

Like a weary traveler on the interstate
desperate for an excuse to stop,
I hesitate between kitchen and front door
tired and already late for work.
Noticing a small marker and plaque,
I pull up at the desk below the window,
"the geographic center of the house,"
or so I crown it with significance.
No Grand Canyon or even Castle Rock,
it serves this traveler's purpose:
the chance for a sip of lukewarm coffee.

An energy exists at the center of things,
the essence of who and what we are.
Sitting on the yellow chair, I pay respect
to a stark landscape unfettered by scenery,
mountain of papers cleared away.
I celebrate the nondescript, not trivial.
Free from expectation, the need to be awed,
I consider the power of emptiness,
stare at the coffee cup ring on the desk.
Closing my eyes, I can feel silence
moving about me like wind through grass.

Breathing deeply, I imagine the people
living in this still section of the house,
contemplative, at times withdrawn,
staring at a horizon of polished wood.
This humble monument is as much for them
as for any geographic distinction,
a testament to pioneer will and fortitude,
reading books and writing poems here
while a television sits in the next room,
ignoring the fridge's incessant pull,
its bright light beaming like Wichita.

The spirit of the place remains indefinable,
locked into wood grain and dim light

streaming from the cracked desk lamp.
Now preparing to hit the road once again,
I gaze at the marker and read the plaque,
jet-black stone serving as paperweight
polished by centuries of wind and storm,
the yellow post-it note attached to wood
with a message from my wife, "Don't be late."
Miles down the road, perhaps feeling lost,
I'll remember this place, the wind and grass

AN EXPATRIATE KANSAN RIDES THE TRAIN OF REMEMBERING

My trip into the vanished past
Is prodded by springs in my seat,
Cracked vinyl scraping an elbow,
And thirst for water, not truth.

This train ain't bound for glory,
Just a slow sixty miles down country,
Through thickets and shorn fields,
Weaving on unsafe tracks.

Today's train ain't no showpiece,
Just an engine and three rusted cars,
Soot seeping through cracks,
Till I wonder what I was thinking

Traveling into Kansas this way,
My life there on that Oswego farm
Surrounded by woods and trees,
The slow trickle of a muddy creek,

Crags below the wooden bridge,
A black hawk circling the hedge,
The farmhouse beyond the hill,
And despite all, enduring love.

I should have gone first class.

DEDICATIONS

Thanks to my creative writing professors for their advice and inspiration, especially Thomas Fox Averill of Washburn University of Topeka and Albert Goldbarth of Wichita State University. Thanks also to Jeanine Hathaway and Anthony Sobin, both of Wichita State University.

Thanks also to Cynthia Pederson and Celia Daniels for their support in publishing my chapbook *Electricity* through Ligature Press.

Thanks to my editor Gary Lechliter for his guidance throughout the process of putting this book together. Also, Pam LeRow provided invaluable assistance in formatting the manuscript.

The Kansas State Historical Society graciously provided permission to use photographs from their collection on the front and back covers.

For many of these poems, especially those in the section "Ghost Town Almanac," I drew inspiration from photographs and captions in several collections: *Kansas: A Pictorial History* by Robert C. Richmond, *Times and Remembrance: A Kansas Legacy* by Bobbie A. Pray, *Reflections of Kansas 1900-1930: A Prairie Postcard Album* by Frank Wood and Scott Daymond, and *The Pioneer Spirit* by Lyle Alan White.

Even more importantly, I drew inspiration from the landscape, people, and history of Kansas, my home state.

This book is for Ruby.

www.ingramcontent.com/pod-product-compliance
Lightning Source LLC
LaVergne TN
LVHW091012080826
845145LV00003B/1237

* 9 7 8 0 9 3 9 3 9 1 4 2 4 *